Design   David West
                Children's Book Design
Editor   Margaret Fagan
Picture researcher   Cecilia Weston-Baker

First published in
the United States in 1990 by
Gloucester Press Inc
387 Park Avenue South
New York NY 10016

The author, Ewan McKay Armstrong, has both medical and health education qualifications. He is a Lecturer in Health Education at South Bank Polytechnic in London, England and has worked both personally and professionally with many people facing the challenge of HIV infection.

© Aladdin Books 1990

Printed in Belgium

Library of Congress Cataloging-in-Publication Data
Armstrong, Ewan McKay.
    The impact of AIDS / Ewan McKay Armstrong
        p. cm. – – (Understanding social issues)
    Summary: Examines the effects of the HIV infection, discusses the efforts in finding a cure for AIDS, and presents case studies of several people who are afflicted with the disease.
        ISBN 0-531-17225-2
    AIDS (Disease) – Social aspects – Juvenile literature.
    [1. AIDS (Disease)]   I. Title   II. Series
    RC 607. A26A76 1990
    362. 1'969792 – – dc20   89–13550 CIP AC

CONTENTS

UNDERSTANDING SOCIAL ISSUES

THE IMPACT OF AIDS

Ewan Armstrong

GLOUCESTER PRESS

New York : London : Toronto : Sydney

AIDS – the Acquired Immune Deficiency Syndrome – has the potential to affect almost every aspect of our lives. Medically, it has challenged health professionals and scientists alike, while the public look on with suspicion.

Of course, the impact of AIDS has not been an easy one to acknowledge. Fears and prejudices have hindered many responses to the crisis and much heartache has been borne of such reactions. Only now are we, in common with other societies across the globe, learning to live with HIV infection in much the same way as we accept other uncertainties in life.

This book is not just about being unwell due to AIDS or HIV (the virus which can cause AIDS). HIV and AIDS itself have forced us to reconsider so many aspects of modern life – for example, how to educate young people, how we worship, make love, plan families and combat illegal drug use. AIDS and HIV have also made people review the politics of providing national health care and worldwide relief programs. That is why it is so important to view both the medical *and* the social impacts of AIDS together. And that is what this book is about.

The impact of AIDS has been felt in three different ways. First of all there are the physical effects of the virus, HIV, and the need to know about practical ways of protecting each other from infection. Secondly, there are the social effects on individuals and communities. And thirdly, there is the effect of AIDS on future generations.

Leaflets from all over the world play a small, but important, part in educating people about the medical and social issues of HIV and AIDS and where to get further help.

CHAPTER 1

WHAT IS HIV INFECTION ? – THE 3 FACTS

While we still don't know how to cure **HIV** infection itself, we do know enough about the virus to prevent it from being passed on – and so protect future generations.

People always want clear facts about something new. Scientists are still doing research on AIDS and a lot of their findings are still too new to be conclusive. However we do know that AIDS is caused by a virus – HIV.

What is a virus?

A virus is one of the smallest germs which can cause an infection by living inside particular cells in plants and animals. There are some viruses which can only live and grow inside human cells and therefore only cause illnesses in humans rather than in other animals.

HIV – the virus which can cause AIDS – grows by living and multiplying inside a human blood cell. Then more new viruses leave this cell to infect – and damage – others.

"I never really thought about it, but I suppose if it was spread like a common cold then we'd all have it."
Home-help

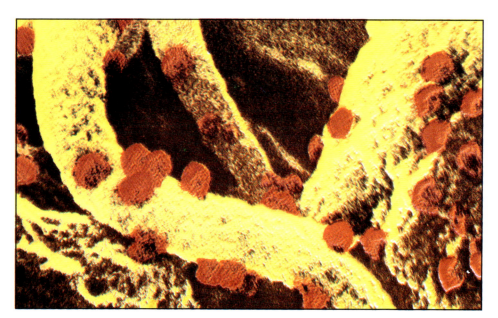

There are many different human viruses, all of which cause completely different illnesses and are passed on in specific ways. For example, the colds most people get at least once a year, which make your nose "run," are caused by viruses passed on through the air we breathe. A virus will only cause an infection if it can reach the specific cells in which it can grow.

HIV – the Human Immunodeficiency Virus – can only cause an infection when it gets inside particular human blood cells – white blood cells. These white cells help give us "immunity" (protection from other germs which might cause illness), and they are found in high concentrations in the body tissues, in the bloodstream itself and in the fluids which are secreted during sex – from a woman's vagina and a man's penis.

It is not these body fluids alone which can pass on the virus from one person to another. They still have to come in direct contact with other living cells in which HIV can live and grow. We now know which activities can do this and how they can be made safer (see overleaf).

At first it was thought that everyone with HIV would eventually become ill within a few years of contracting the virus. However, scientists now have a more optimistic outlook: many people have had HIV for at least 10 years and have not shown any physical signs of the infection. Because many people with HIV are unaware that they have the virus and do not show any symptoms, we cannot rely on being able to recognize who is "risky" or safe. Instead, we need to know how to avoid the risk of infection.

The THREE Facts!

HIV can be passed from person to person in three specific ways, as shown in the box below.

HIV can be passed from one person to another –

- **during sex**   – **if it is anal or vaginal intercourse without using a condom, if one of the partners is infected**

- **during injections**   – **if infected blood is injected and if infected ("dirty") needles and syringes are shared**

- **during pregnancy**   – **if a woman has HIV infection her baby in the womb might also become infected**

HIV cannot be passed from one person to another –

- **during eating, playing, sleeping, hugging, kissing, talking, dancing.........in fact it CANNOT be passed on during most things we do!**

In these three ways HIV can reach and infect the white blood cells in which it grows and lives. It is highly unlikely that it can cause an infection in any other way. No one has become infected with HIV through everyday social contact with someone with the virus, whether shaking hands or hugging, whether traveling on the same bus or train, eating in the same restaurant, working in the same room or swimming in the same pool. People have asked lots of questions about other activities: do activities like kissing, cleaning a grazed knee, giving first aid like the "kiss of life" spread HIV infection? As time has passed, *no* new information has supported the idea that these are likely ways of passing on HIV.

How widespread is the problem?

Over the years a large number of people world-wide (over 175,000 by September 1989) have been reported with AIDS. But this official figure (from the World Health Organization – WHO) is probably much lower than the real number of people with AIDS, and the number of people who have HIV, but are still well, is undoubtedly much larger. No one knows exactly how many people "carry" the virus (HIV) which causes AIDS. WHO calculates that 450,000 people have AIDS and estimates that five to ten million people carry the virus worldwide.

Sharing "dirty" needles or syringes with someone who has the virus is a very efficient way of spreading HIV, and drug users must be helped to reduce their risks. Needle exchange programs which offer clean needles for used needles aim to prevent HIV from spreading.

Testing for HIV

Many people only know that they have HIV because they have had a test. There is a good deal of controversy about testing for HIV and no one should be tested without adequate counseling first. If the results of the test are positive, then an individual is faced with the uncertainty of not knowing whether he or she will eventually become ill with AIDS, and many find this an extremely difficult burden to live with.

> "I haven't had the test because of fear – I suppose it's fear of the unknown. I really don't know how I would handle the situation if I was found to be positive."
> Office worker

Some people choose to be tested because they need the information to make clear decisions. They may need to know if they are HIV positive in order to make changes in their lives, like practicing safe sex to protect themselves and others. One young man, Mark, who used to inject drugs, wanted to start a family and so decided to have a test. He went to his local Sexually Transmitted Diseases (STD) Clinic and talked with a counselor for a long time before he decided to go ahead with the test. The counselor discussed with him the many different considerations: what if the test was positive, what effect would knowing this have on Mark and Linda, his wife? The counselor talked to Mark and Linda about the implications a positive result could have on their hopes of having children and on their sex life. If Mark's results were positive, should they begin to practice safe sex and use a condom instead of the contraceptive pill in case Linda didn't carry HIV? Should Linda have the test also? And if they decided to go ahead and try to have a child, what were the chances of their child having AIDS at birth..?

What do they test for?

The HIV test is not a test for the actual virus, but it tests for "HIV antibodies" in the blood, special chemicals our bodies make a few weeks or months after becoming infected with HIV. These "antibodies" are a sign that the person has been infected with HIV and that they still carry the virus so that they may be a risk to others in the three ways outlined above. The fact that it takes some time from infection with the virus for the body to make antibodies means that someone could have the

Using her media coverage, the Princess of Wales has helped to calm fears about social contact with people with HIV and AIDS.

Telephone helplines are anonymous and confidential, and many people prefer to talk with an experienced phone advisor about their concerns before going to a doctor or clinic.

virus, but still be tested as "antibody negative."

"He just slipped this bit of paper under the glass screen. I couldn't understand all the boxes on the form until eventually I worked it out – "negative." I was so shocked – god knows what it's like if you're positive."
Young man, living in New York

Feeling unwell

Many other people only find out that they have HIV infection because they develop physical symptoms or feel unwell. Veronica had been well until she noticed what looked like a bruise on her foot, and the doctor at the clinic confirmed her fears that it was an AIDS-related tumor. It hasn't gone away, but she has stayed well otherwise.

HIV damages the body's immunity to certain other germs which would not normally cause serious problems in healthy people. The virus lives in human white cells and multiplies, making more and more of itself. The virus-infected cells die prematurely as a result of infection. As this goes on, fewer and fewer white cells are able to protect the human body from these other germs and people can become very ill with these other infections.

Scientists check and double check HIV antibody tests under strict laboratory conditions.

"There was a time when every time I felt tired or had a sore throat, I was sure I had AIDS. I even convinced myself to have a test. Now I know it was just a guilty conscience."
Business man, 32

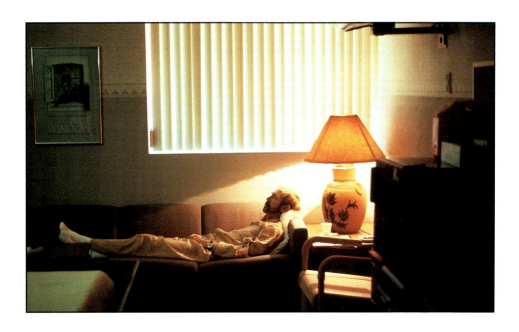

People with AIDS need a variety of services – like this community hospital – to support them through periods of illness and convalescence.

Symptoms of HIV infection

At first, someone might feel slightly unwell and they may notice that their glands swell up in different parts of their body. However, this general feeling of ill-health is often no more than a bad cold, or the "flu" – or just being "run down." But for someone with HIV, these symptoms might be the first signs of infection. People whose immunity is more seriously damaged by HIV could show signs of a number of different diseases, including pneumonia, diarrhea, skin infections and tumors, and brain diseases, all of which affect people in different ways.

Each person shows the first signs of becoming ill in a different way – the onset of AIDS does not follow a set pattern. However, if a person receives treatment for the infection they may not feel unwell again for a number of months or years.

"Is there a test for AIDS itself?"
The short answer is "No!" AIDS is a "syndrome," a pattern of several medical problems at once. AIDS can only be recognized by a doctor examining someone known to have HIV infection already. There is, therefore, no single test for AIDS itself.

Other beliefs about the cause of AIDS
Experts now agree that someone must have HIV infection for such medical problems as AIDS and ARC (AIDS-Related Complex) to develop. This was not always the only view. For example, before HIV was identified, some people thought that AIDS was caused by people "living in the fast lane." Others suggested that the human body can be "overloaded" with several untreated infections at the same time, wearing out the supply of white cells.

> **"AIDS is part of the fruits of the permissive society. The regular one-man one-woman marriage would not put us at risk of this in any way."** Journalist

History of a Disease –	
1981	AIDS first recognized in the United States
1982/3	AIDS-Related Complex recognized
1983/4	The virus discovered, and named, at the same time in – France (called LAV) and the United States (called HTLV III)
1986	The virus renamed HIV
1988	The range of illnesses renamed HIV Disease

"Why do most scientists agree on HIV?"

You might think that it is only scientists in white coats who find out about new diseases, and indeed much of what we know about HIV comes from laboratory investigations with the virus itself. But another source of information about the virus, how it is passed on and the illnesses it causes, is through the study of groups of people or communities. This study of disease in populations (rather than studying just one person at a time) is called epidemiology. The patterns which it reveals provide important clues which, together with laboratory results, give a clear picture of the likely causes and effects of disease.

This is how AIDS was investigated and, whatever you believe about the cause, advice about prevention remains the same: practice safe sex or make intercourse safer by using a condom proper-

Amongst other things, the 1980s will be remembered for the promotion of the condom as just another fact of life.

ly, and if you do inject illegal drugs always use a clean needle and syringe.

Advice about what is safe sex or the dangers of drug use may not always seem easily available. For example, Todd goes regularly to a youth club where they have just installed two new condom dispensing machines in the bathrooms. This means that anyone who attends the youth club can buy condoms if they need them. But Todd has heard a few "jokes" about the kind of people who use "rubbers." And some of the people at the club have started to brag about having sex without using a condom.

Fortunately, the youth club workers have planned to discuss the new machines, and why it is important to know how to use a condom effectively, with groups of club members in the next few weeks. They hope that this will help people to understand that sexual intercourse without using a condom is very risky. They hope too it will help people to talk about their embarrassment about sex and the surrounding issues of their relationships.

> "My boyfriend doesn't mind buying my tampons as long as I buy the condoms: it's odd the way people get so embarrassed about it all."
> Tina, aged 18

The youth club workers are also planning to hold discussion groups on the problems of using drugs and have made sure that there are plenty of pamphlets and posters explaining to people all the issues involved.

CHAPTER 2

PEOPLE
WITH
AIDS
&
HIV

People with **AIDS**
are men and
women,
young and old,
white and black,
heterosexual
and homosexual,
interesting
and boring –
like you and me.

Look around you next time you're in a busy street or on a crowded bus. You can often tell some things about people just by looking at them or listening carefully. But you can't tell just by looking at someone if they have HIV. Potentially any of us could be at risk at some time or another and it's up to us all to protect ourselves.

> **"An awful lot of calls start – I'm a happily married man, but……"**
> AIDS helpline advisor

Who has AIDS?

At the moment most people with AIDS in the United States are gay men. This is also true in Britain. However, if we look at the effects of AIDS in particular cities in each of these two countries, the pattern is more complicated. According to recent statistics, AIDS is the biggest cause of death for women aged between 25 and 34 in New York City. And while in London most people with AIDS are gay men, in Edinburgh, Scotland, they are mostly heterosexual men and women who have become infected through injecting illegal drugs.

> **"The danger of AIDS to the heterosexual is still widely ignored or disbelieved."**
> AIDS expert

A woman with HIV and her baby both face an uncertain future and will need the best care available, and the support of friends and family.

Today, the pattern of people who become infected with HIV has changed compared to ten years ago, when the epidemic was just beginning. In Europe and North America the rate of new cases of HIV in gay men is actually decreasing.

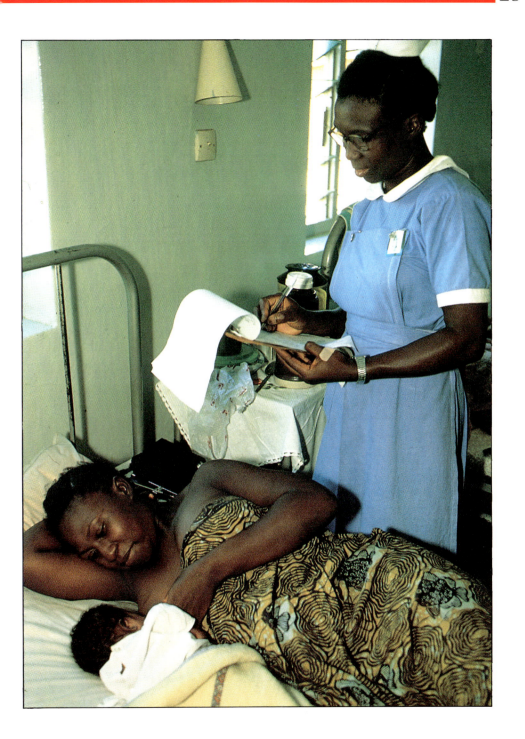

This is because gay groups have been involved in educating themselves about HIV and AIDS, learning from the experience of supporting friends who have become ill or died, and changing their behavior. Today, heterosexual men and women are the fastest growing group affected by HIV in the United States and in Europe. Many heterosexual people either do not know enough about HIV infection, or think that it has nothing to do with them, and are unaware how to protect themselves. A different pattern has been seen in some African countries since the start of the epidemic, where men and women have been affected in almost equal proportions.

Babies and children with HIV infection
Babies and children can also have HIV infection and AIDS. They become infected either before birth, across the mother's placenta, or possibly after birth through breast milk. Whereas adults with HIV can stay healthy for a long time, babies born with HIV become unwell in a matter of months or years, sometimes dying very young. Parents of babies with HIV and AIDS often have the virus themselves and need a lot of support and good hospital services to help them look after their children.

"You never know what will happen. I don't like to think about it, but I have to face the fact that some day he may fall ill. That's where the uncertainty is." Mother of a young boy with HIV

In the United States, where the heterosexual spread of HIV is especially affecting the under-privileged, three-quarters of all children with AIDS are black or hispanic.

Having a family raises particular questions for women with HIV – "Will my baby be born with the virus?", "Should I breastfeed?" and "Will I become sick when I'm pregnant?"

"To date, 92% of the 250 children in New York who have developed AIDS have been born to ethnic minority mothers."
The PANOS Institute, 1988

A smaller number of older children have HIV because they have been given a blood transfusion or other medical treatment which was unknowingly infected with HIV. This is particularly true for hemophiliac children, who have an inherited blood disease which needs to be treated with blood products. Like adults, older children with HIV may stay well for long periods of time and can go to school and play sports.

Meeting needs

Everyone who has AIDS needs the same resources, and these are similar to the requirements of any healthy person. We all need food and water, we need a roof over our heads and warmth and security, and we need love and friendship. Beyond these, we all want to do interesting things with our lives and have a sense of purpose and belonging. People with AIDS need these things like everyone else; perhaps they even need them more urgently to help them to stay well.

Living with AIDS means different things to different people, but independence can be very important. The basics of life go on, like going shopping and socializing.

Eating well

People with AIDS who eat a nutritious diet, well-prepared in hygienic surroundings, can boost their own immunity to help keep themselves well.

Many people lose their appetite and a high calorie diet of appetizing food can help them keep up their weight. Fresh food might need to be bought every day, and, if a person with AIDS is living on their own, volunteers and friends can play an important role in doing the shopping. However, this assumes that fresh, nutritious food is available and that a person can afford to buy it, which is not always the case in either rich or poor countries.

Where to live

Throughout the world homelessness, especially in big cities, is a serious social issue, and finding adequate accommodation to rent is increasingly difficult. Many people with AIDS are evicted from their homes by unsympathetic landlords, or harassed by neighbors who, wrongly, fear close social contact with them. Mortgages are almost impossible to get with the current restrictions imposed by life insurance companies who are not prepared to insure people with HIV or AIDS.

"I've only been back home twice since all the hassle. I'm afraid that someone will recognize me and take a shot – or even torch Dad's house."
Young man with AIDS

It can be difficult to find a house which is suitable for a person who may suffer from periods of physical weakness. However, many authorities now realize that it is both cheaper and preferable to keep someone in their own home when they are ill, and most social service departments in London

Some projects now provide special accommodation for people with AIDS to recover from a period of illness or for experienced terminal care. This room at London Lighthouse is a comfortable place for friends, family and residents to meet away from the bedside.

now train all their staff to be able to work well with clients with AIDS.

"**Even though we're on the top floor, it's quieter at home and at least I can rest whenever I want.**"
Person with AIDS

A number of projects have been set up to help people with HIV and AIDS who have nowhere suitable to stay. For example, the SHANTI Project has been funded by the City of San Francisco to provide group homes, where several people with the virus live together. Drug users or ex-users can often find it particularly difficult to get a secure home. Some projects are being set up where they will be supported to come off drugs at the same time.

Emotional support

Perhaps the most obvious worry for anyone with HIV infection is how to cope with the uncertainty of whether or not they will become ill and dependent on other people. Most hospitals have people who will talk with clients about the implications of HIV and of the test – and most self-help organizations also provide counseling services to help people get through the first shock and support them to keep well.

Spiritual health

Many religious people support people with HIV and AIDS, individually and through community projects. This is important for those who believe in a healthy mind, body *and* spirit.

But some people still believe that AIDS is the "wrath of God" – that God has punished particular groups of people, like gay men, for sinning. Other religious people hold to the doctrine of "love the sinner, hate the sin." This allows them to support people who are unwell without supporting all aspects of their lifestyles.

> **"They say they love God, but people who love God shouldn't do this."**
> Christian woman whose brother has AIDS

Reactions of friends and family

Being told that you have AIDS affects everyone near and dear to you. People's reactions range from total rejection to wholehearted support. Sometimes their reaction depends on how the person became infected – the "innocent or guilty" response. For example, babies with HIV have been called the "innocent victims," somehow implying that other people are "guilty victims" who deserved to get HIV. This division of reactions is particularly true when people talk about drug users with HIV.

Positively healthy

A nurse takes time to talk and listen with a young man at London Lighthouse. In the busy world of health care, these are skills which need much more attention for the benefit of staff and patients alike.

Most people with HIV learn to live with the uncertainty and still maintain a sense of hope, especially now that new treatments seem to make a difference. Many people have taken part in scientific drug experiments and have benefited from the drugs used. One drug, Zidovudine (AZT), has given new hope that HIV can be prevented from growing inside human blood cells, at least until side effects occur.

Even more people have tried a variety of complimentary health care approaches, from acupuncture and homeopathy to relaxation techniques, and have found them useful.

Death and dying

People die with AIDS. When you're 15 or 16 death seems a very long way off – not something you need to think about. Talking about dying can be very upsetting, but it is important for people with HIV to be able to talk with family and friends when they want to, especially because they don't know when they might become ill. Organizing practical things, such as making a will, can actually help people to get on with living. When someone knows they are dying, they may say the things they really feel, and do the things they have always wanted to.

Hopelessness can severely affect a person's health. Even when someone becomes acutely ill, they need support and encouragement.

"After the examination, two young doctors came in and explained about the pneumonia and that I was HIV antibody positive. They said I only had a couple of weeks to live. That was months ago and I'm really surprised to be alive this year. I didn't fall apart. In fact, I was really pleased they'd told me the truth – it helped me to cope."
Person with AIDS

People with AIDS have adopted the shorthand "PWA" to ensure that they are referred to as people first and foremost, rather than being described only in terms of their illness.

When David first discovered he had HIV, some years ago, he was convinced that the best way to cope was to carry on as usual. As he wasn't in a sexual relationship with anyone, David thought this course of action would be easy to follow. Yet, the strain of keeping his anxieties secret began to show. Eventually, David began to talk about his worries to a few people. Their reactions quickly proved to him that he did indeed have a handful of trustworthy friends who didn't withdraw because of his news.

David has now become ill and relies on his friends to help him with daily chores. The nurses who are also involved in caring for David have all been concerned with far more than just his physical condition. Fortunately, David's fear that people would see him only in terms of his illness has not been his experience.

CASE STUDY

Paul is 27 years old and lives with his boyfriend, Mario, in London. Paul found out that he had HIV four years ago and he was well until about six months ago when he developed a persistent cough and started to lose weight. They went to the hospital and the doctor examined him, listening to his breathing and looking at X rays. The results all pointed to a particular kind of pneumonia and he was admitted to the "AIDS ward" for immediate treatment. Paul had suddenly become a person with AIDS, and he felt like just another statistic.

Mario was very worried about Paul and whether or not he would live. Every day he came after work with stories of friends and family and colleagues. But sometimes they preferred not to talk, but just held hands and didn't say anything. The drug Paul was getting had to be continually fed into his bloodstream and so he was always connected up to a "drip" on a tall stand. After a week or so on treatment, Mario arrived and found Paul walking around the ward, dragging his "drip" behind him!

Soon afterward Paul was well enough to go home and he now takes several pills a day to stop him from getting ill again. So far he has stayed well, and he has put on so much weight that he has had to buy new trousers to fit. He isn't working anymore, as he gets tired very easily. Going for a walk with Mario or meeting friends are what he likes best.

In the past few weeks, Paul's parents have been to stay with them and this has meant a lot to Paul. However, it's not been easy for his mom and dad to accept his relationship with Mario or his illness. They have been supported by parents of other people with AIDS, two of whom traveled a long way to meet them and discuss their respective situations. They also recently attended a weekend course to help them understand what to expect if Paul becomes ill again.

Friends, family and a variety of different professionals are all now involved in supporting Paul and Mario. But most of all they have each other.

CHAPTER 3

GLOBAL ISSUES

We are slowly
moving away
from
the narrow view
that **HIV**
infection
& **AIDS** is some
other country's
problem to a
broader "global"
picture which
requires a
worldwide
response.

In the late 19th century, most responses to the sexually transmitted disease syphilis were based on prejudice rather than on knowledge of the germ which causes it.

Doctors first started to treat people with AIDS in 1981. Before long, some newspapers started to ask "who was to blame?" and some people held views that bore no relation to the facts.

> **"I read that it was probably released by mistake from one of those germ warfare places – I wouldn't put it past them."**
> Social worker

Blaming other countries

The popular press has certainly played a large part in whipping up fears surrounding AIDS and the groups of people affected by it. The newspapers sensationalize stories of "AIDS victims" as hopeless, weak, or just plain bad. AIDS has been used by newspapers to show their readers that their prejudices against homosexuals or drug users are justified. But blaming others is not a new story. The same thing happened when another sexually transmitted disease (STD) called syphilis became widespread. About 100 years ago, when there was a marked rise in the number of people with this infection (an epidemic), different countries coined names for it which put blame on others – in France it was called "the English disease" while in England it was known as "the French disease."

"Each time a story or TV program goes out, the phones don't stop – and mostly they're from "The Worried Well" – people who haven't put themselves at risk of infection at all."
AIDS Helpline Advisor

As more people became ill with AIDS worldwide, doctors and epidemiologists soon found that it didn't matter which group, community or country people came from, only what they did. The idea that gay men or people who injected illegal drugs were the *only* groups at risk was simply not true. Today, no one can assume that they are immune from HIV infection, yet many heterosexual people behave as if this were the case – for example, many don't consider practicing safer sex because they feel they belong to a "safe" group. This is a dangerous way to think: while people argue about "risk groups" they may continue to take risks – and some will become infected.

A celebration of civil rights in New York is joined by people advertising the positive message "We are surviving AIDS," giving hope to others and challenging media images of people with AIDS.

Stopping the epidemic

As countries became more aware of the potential size of the AIDS epidemic, many reacted by setting up restrictions designed to keep out potential "HIV carriers." Some countries have responded by thinking about testing all people coming into the country to see if they carry HIV antibodies.

Indeed, some politicians and newspapers suggested that all Africans immigrating to Britain should be tested for HIV. This was shown to be based only on racism (discrimination against people because of color) since no similar suggestion was made for people immigrating from any other part of the world. Many other countries, like China, Greece, India, Libya, Saudi Arabia and Poland all require "negative certificates" from foreign students entering the country.

However, these kinds of restrictions probably won't stop the spread of HIV – such measures won't prevent entry to people with HIV who don't know they have the virus and whose bodies have not yet made antibodies to HIV.

Effects on whole populations

As more young men, women and babies become infected with HIV, the population of some countries may actually fall over the next ten years, and this will have serious effects on the wealth of these countries. Some countries which rely on tourism to bring in money and to support jobs fear that tourists will stop visiting due to worries about HIV and AIDS. If this happened at the same time as large numbers of the population needed expensive medical care, the problem could be critical and add financial costs to the human ones.

Capturing the public attention, the Ugandan Government Minister of Health promotes safer sex by giving out free condoms and leaflets as part of health education.

> "Worldwide, it seems likely that a new person becomes infected with HIV every minute."
> The PANOS Institute, 1988

World health

In 1986, the World Health Organization (WHO) set up a new project ("Global Program on AIDS" – GPA) devoted to a worldwide response to HIV infection and AIDS. The GPA spends nearly $100 million each year; some of this money comes from rich countries, like the United States, and is given to support education and health services in poorer countries.

> "In some central African hospitals one-quarter to one-third of scarce hospital beds are occupied by AIDS patients."
> WHO Official

Total Number of People with AIDS –

Officially Reported Worldwide
Up to 1980 59
Up to 1989 (September) 177,965

Actual Number Estimated Worldwide
Up to 1989 480,000

Expected Number Worldwide
By 1991 1,000,000

Many countries have a large number of people with HIV and few resources for adequate health care. They lack drugs to treat the infections which people with AIDS get, and even simple hygienic equipment, such as disposable gloves, syringes and needles, is in short supply and costs too much for many countries to pay for themselves.

Some people still question the need to spend so much time and energy on a single health issue. Hopefully, "working together" will also benefit other health programs, such as family planning, rather than divert energy away from them.

> **"In most countries the number of AIDS cases doubles about every 10 months."**
> World health expert

Governments are also setting up educational projects which will prepare their population for the effects of HIV in 10 or 20 years time. Unless a vaccine is produced and made available to all countries within the next few years (and this is now unlikely), we will all depend solely on education to

Health educators in Uganda are keen to use classroom discussions to help put AIDS education into practice.

protect ourselves and others from HIV.

"Even though the United States still has had more people with AIDS than anywhere else in the world put together, African and Caribbean countries face a relatively larger problem for the size of population."
Epidemiologist

The difference between HIV and AIDS
Some people are confused about the differences between AIDS and HIV. They talk about people with HIV and people with AIDS as if there was no distinction, but it is important to distinguish between the two. The official number of people with reported cases of AIDS is still quite low (less that 200,000), but this figure is artificially low for a number of reasons. First of all, some people with AIDS have not been reported as having AIDS because some doctors are reluctant to label patients in this way – they know about the problems it may cause, including discrimination, in many areas of life. Secondly, for every person with AIDS there are many more people who carry the virus, but who stay well. This means that the figure of nearly 200,000 represents only the tip of an iceberg – there are many more people that already carry HIV and who will become unwell in ten to fifteen years time.

Another reason for the inaccurately low number of reported cases of AIDS is the fact that many countries do not have a developed health care system. In some places there may not be the

resources to adequately register all those who are ill, or their illness may go undiagnosed.

Globally, we are balancing the two aspects of the epidemic – developing services for people who are already ill while educating everyone about HIV infection, high-risk behavior and ways of staying healthy by protecting ourselves and others.

There is also a great deal more research that still needs to be done to understand the spread of the epidemic. For example, one large-scale survey which is about to be carried out in Britain will eventually provide information about the different sexual practices that people have. This will help health educators to use the medical facts about HIV infection in more effective ways. Social and medical research go hand in hand to broaden our understanding of both the disease itself and its wide-ranging effects.

Family doctors need to be educated about the social impact of AIDS too, as in this teaching session led by a British AIDS counselor.

CHAPTER 4

COMMUNITY RESPONSES

**Ironically it
has been those
people most
affected who
have shown
us all how to
live with the
uncertainty
of HIV infection.**

There isn't an area of life that hasn't been touched in some way by issues raised by HIV. AIDS, as a social issue, has challenged so many things we've taken for granted, from basic hygiene and good hospital practice, to sex and drug education, from "gay rights" to "third world" poverty.

While some authorities still ignore the relevance of HIV, others are investigating the changes they need to make to face up to the impact of HIV. Schools and colleges, factories and offices, governments and churches have also started to question how they relate to HIV and AIDS.

This little boy with AIDS faces an uncertain future. And he will be growing up in a world which must also face uncertainties and learn how best to cope with them.

Schools

In the United States some children with HIV infection have been banned from local schools even after a legal judgment has stated that they should be allowed to attend classes there. Not

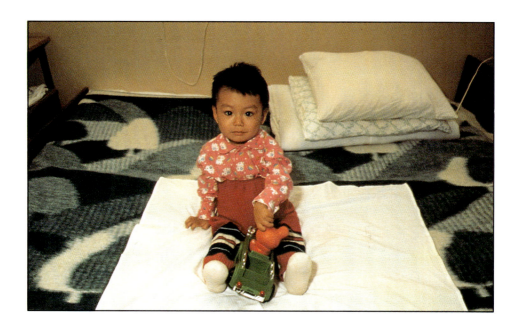

surprisingly, parents may decide not to tell teachers or other parents that their child has HIV, fearing that they might get the same response.

Some schools may have turned their backs on children with HIV, but others have been reassured that there is no risk of infection in the fun of the playground.

> "In the state of Florida, the three HIV-positive sons of a hemophiliac family were barred from attending class by school authorities, and their house was burned by arsonists."
> AIDS worker

Some schools only started to think about AIDS when faced with such a situation. But others have reviewed school policy and practice before any such situation could arise.

Sex and drugs.....
Educating people about safe sex and drug use to

prevent the spread of HIV has aroused a lot of controversy. Sex and drugs are difficult subjects to talk about openly and people have strong feelings about how these subjects should be introduced. Some schools have taken the approach that *all* sex is dangerous, all drugs addictive, and that all you have to do to avoid HIV is "just say No." A different approach is to introduce discussion about HIV infection across school activities – in the biology class, during a geography lesson and when discussing religion. Whichever approach your school takes, teachers have to prepare themselves to answer questions; on sex, drugs, HIV itself, and many others, and they may feel embarrassed or be ignorant themselves.

HIV education at school involves more than simply giving "the facts," but means exploring what they mean to young people today.

In Britain, the situation has been made more difficult by a new law which has banned "the promotion of homosexuality" by local authorities

and some people have used this law as an excuse not to talk about homosexuality at all. However, many school boards have agreed a consistent approach to sex education and HIV with the support of teachers and parents.

Churches

We often look to religious leaders for guidance on modern-day issues, such as divorce and contraception. This poses a problem for many religious people when considering HIV and AIDS. Religions all over the world have been forced to discuss the impact of HIV infection on the way we live our lives. Many pastoral care projects have been set up to help people affected by HIV infection and to educate church members. No one religion has come up with any easy answers about HIV and AIDS and some of the discussion has

Individual church members and clergy are important carers for people with AIDS who have spiritual beliefs.

even divided people within religions themselves.

Self-help and voluntary groups

The discrimination faced by people with AIDS and HIV has taken many forms: they have found themselves shunned by family or friends, without a doctor, a job or a secure home at a time when they may be trying to cope with serious ill-health. Because of this, people affected by HIV have worked together to help themselves. For example, people with the blood disease hemophilia, who became infected through medical injections, have gained a lot of support from others in the same situation. Frontliners is a British organization of people with AIDS which gives advice and support to others. Like Body Positive, a self-help group for people with HIV, it grew out of the Terrence Higgins Trust which provides a range of HIV-related services in London.

The NAMES Project, based in San Francisco, is a different kind of group. It provides a focus for people to remember friends and relatives through what is now the largest community arts project in the United States. The end product is a huge quilt, made up of thousands of small panels sewn together each in memory of someone who has died with AIDS. It has been used to symbolize the human cost of AIDS. Organizations like "Frontliners" in Britain and "People with AIDS Coalition" in the United States have put the human face on this health issue in a way that no one else can. Perhaps no other health issue has motivated so many people affected by it to become involved in shaping the services developed worldwide.

Working together

Many of the people most affected by HIV so far have been actively involved in educating populations worldwide, criticizing some government policies and supporting others. This was necessary because some officials such as politicians, teachers and doctors, were initially reluctant to be involved, sometimes refusing to recognize the seriousness of the AIDS epidemic. This was probably due in part to their own fears. But now many are in the frontline of care and education and have learned more about HIV and those affected.

One feature which marks the global response to HIV infection is the way professionals and people with HIV and AIDS are working closely together to develop appropriate services for a variety of different groups of people in the light of changing circumstances and information.

Burning candles of remembrance highlights the sorrow of people affected in different ways by HIV and AIDS.

CASE STUDY

Jon and Mary were married for three years before they had their first child, Kelly. Mary had a blood transfusion, but neither of them knew at the time that it had given her HIV infection. But when Kelly became ill just after her fourth birthday, doctors discovered that she had AIDS.

In the meantime Mary and Jon had had a son, Kevin. After Kelly's health improved, all the family were tested, and only Jon tested negative.

Mary has never felt physically unwell herself with HIV, but the strain of worrying about her children and the guilt she feels, even though there was nothing she could do, is almost unbearable at times.

The staff at the hospital were wonderful, but some "friends" stopped phoning a few months ago when a local newspaper found out about them and ran a story about "The AIDS Family Next Door." Kelly was looking forward to school, but some of her friends' parents complained to the school authorities and Mary and Jon had difficulty finding one that would take her.

They moved to a new area and both children are now at schools which know and accept that they have HIV. Mary is now keeping well with the help of new medications.

Jon and Mary have recently met other parents facing the same challenges and are learning to live each day as it comes, with hope.

But more than anything else, both Jon and Mary have gained a great deal from being able to educate other parents and local professional groups, drawing on their own painful experiences. Their hope is that this will make a difference to other families who will have to face similar challenges.

Both Kelly and Kevin are enjoying their new schools and school friends. And Kelly particularly enjoys the new experience of swimming and has become a frequent visitor to the local swimming pool. Her next big day is coming up soon – a party for her fifth birthday. She has invited many of her school friends and has helped her mother to bake the cake.

CASE STUDY

Fiona is a 22 year-old woman with HIV. Last month her world fell apart when she became ill with "blood poisoning." She was taken by a friend to the Accident & Emergency department of the local city hospital. The doctors quickly transferred her to the special "AIDS ward" when they recognized the injection marks on her body and when she told them of her heroin addiction.

Treating the blood infection was relatively easy, but the HIV antibody test came back positive and other tests showed that she had had other infections and swollen glands. Fiona had put these symptoms down to her drug habit, but now she was facing the possibility that these were AIDS-related illnesses.

When the doctors asked her about injecting drugs she told them about the few times she had shared "works" – needles and syringes – maybe six times at the most, out of sheer desperation. But she had also had intercourse with her boyfriend many times over the last year and he had always laughed when she asked him to use a condom.

Whichever way she actually became infected, Fiona is now looking to the future, and how to keep herself as well as possible. Unfortunately, her family and her boyfriend have refused to visit her or even send cards or flowers. But new friends, particularly through the local "Women & AIDS" support group, have helped her make plans for when she gets out of the hospital. The last thing she wants now is to meet up with people she used to know through her drug habit, so she's trying to find a new place to live. And she is looking for a Drug Rehabilitation Project in another part of the country to break her addiction and to help her make a new start.

Fiona's experiences have shaken her – she often feels daunted by the prospect of "starting a new life." But with the help of the local support group, she has realized that sharing her experiences can help others to understand more about their drug problems. She is also considering going on a course to learn basic computing once she has found a new place to live.

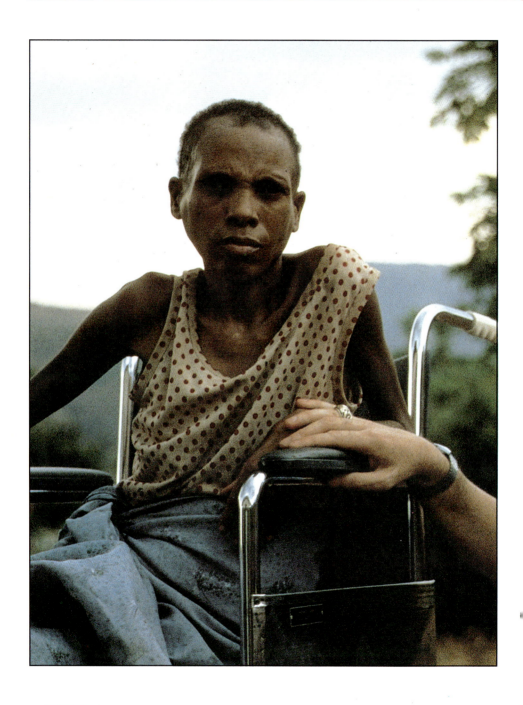

CHAPTER 5

FACING
THE
FUTURE

No single avenue
should be
explored
at the expense of
others – the more
ways of coping,
the more options
we'll all have
to choose from.

As we find out more and more about HIV and AIDS it is not the medical facts which become more complicated – these are now quite clear – but the social effects of this new disease are expanding almost every day. Two overlapping areas of investigation are now being carried out – how to control the medical problems caused by HIV and how to live with the social ones.

The search for a cure

New treatments and vaccines are being investigated every day across the globe. But experts agree that neither a cure nor an effective vaccine are yet in sight.

Unfortunately, a cure for HIV infection is not just around the corner. A lot of money has been spent by large drug companies to find the one drug which will kill the virus in the bloodstream, but without any success so far. Old drugs, used to treat other diseases, are being tried and new drugs are being made all the time. But even if a promising drug was found tomorrow, it would be many years

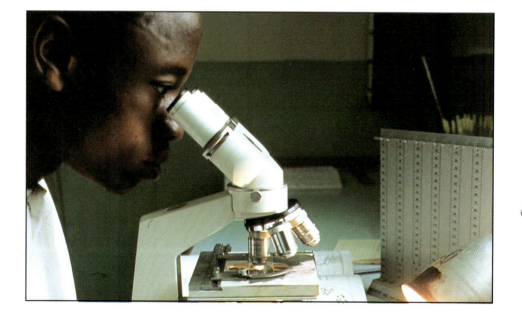

before it could be used widely. First it would have to be tried and tested on a few people and the results carefully compared to the progress of people who hadn't been treated with the drug.

> **"I don't expect that they will find a cure in my lifetime – but I hope to God there will be one in time for my children."**
> Women with AIDS, mother of two children with HIV

One drug, Zidovudine (or AZT), is the most promising so far. It stops HIV growing and multiplying, although it doesn't kill it completely. People with HIV do stay well for longer if they take this drug although it can cause other medical problems itself.

Many other scientists are researching into a vaccine which would protect us from the virus before becoming infected. However, it is difficult to make a vaccine against HIV and a widely available one is a long way off. Ultimately, this is preferable to a cure since it is bound to be much less expensive and will be less likely to cause serious side effects.

Health Education

Prevention is always better than a cure. Since a vaccine is not going to be available for some years, health education about HIV and AIDS is vitally important. We need to think about HIV infection in relation to all aspects of our lives – at school, our likes and dislikes, our future plans, our boyfriends and girlfriends. As we grow older, our lives will

If future generations are still to enjoy the excitement of discovery – without putting each other at any long-term risks – then older generations must respond with calm creativity.

change and we must be able to change our attitudes toward health too. Because HIV can lie dormant for such a long period of time, health education has to encourage people who appear healthy to change their behavior.

"**What the government ads failed to get over is the time lag between getting infected and becoming ill.**"
Health Education Officer

The next decade with AIDS
A worldwide effort to cope with HIV and AIDS is now under way. Each school, town, city and country is facing up to AIDS in different ways. Perhaps the most we can expect is a positive, forward-looking approach which challenges discrimination and which, above all else, is caring.

But as we approach the year 2000, we must keep up with developments. People need clear, consistent, up-to-date information, simply presented and unaffected by prejudice; educational programs must acknowledge cultural attitudes, helping societies and individuals to learn from each other.

In the face of a global tragedy, the impact of AIDS can never be said to be a positive one. But perhaps it will help us to understand other social issues better, to protect ourselves and to prepare for the future.

The NAMES Project quilt continues to grow. It is both a remembrance of the effects of AIDS over the past decade and a constant reminder to all of us to safeguard the future.

"For better or worse, what we do in the 1990s will continue to have an enormous impact well into the 21st century. The future really is in our own hands."
AIDS Educator

SOURCES OF HELP

Your family doctor may be able to help with general enquiries about HIV and your health. If you're worried about going to him or her, or would like to talk to someone anonymously, you can contact any of the organizations below.

Centers for Disease Control (CDC)
AIDS Activity
Building 6, Room 274
1600 Clifton Road, NE
Atlanta, GA 30333
Telephone (404) 329-2891
National Toll-Free Hotline
1-800-342-AIDS (recorded information)

American Social Health Association
National AIDS Hotline
P.O. Box 1274
New York, NY 10113
Toll-Free Hotline
1-800-342-7514 (for specific questions)

AIDS Action Council
Federation of AIDS-Related
Organizations
729 8th Street, SE
Washington, DC 20003
Telephone (202) 547-3101

National Institute of Allergy and Infectious Diseases
Office of Communications
Building 31, Room 7A32
National Institutes of Health
9000 Rockville Pike
Bethesda, MD 20892
Telephone (301) 496-5717

Health Crisis Network
P.O. Box 52-1546
Miami, Florida 33152
(305) 634-4636

San Francisco Aids Foundation
4th Floor
333 Valencia Street
San Francisco, California 94103
(415) 864-4376

AIDS Project
Oak Lawn Counseling Center
3000 Turtle Creek Plaza
Suite 116
Dallas, Texas 75219
(214) 520-8108

AIDS Prevention
151 Eleventh Avenue
South Charleston,
West Virginia 25303
1-(800(642-8244

WHAT THE WORDS MEAN

AIDS Acquired Immune Deficiency Syndrome

anal intercourse sex in which a man's penis is put into his partner's anus

antibody positive what someone is said to be if their test shows that they have HIV infection

antibody a specific chemical made in the body to neutralize or destroy a virus or germ that has invaded it

condom a rubber or latex sheath put over a man's penis during sex to prevent infection or pregnancy

epidemic a widespread outbreak of a disease, attacking great numbers of people in one place at one time, and which can travel from place to place

gay man a man who has male sexual partners; homosexual

hemophilia a disease which is passed on in families in which the blood does not clot easily

HIV Human Immunodeficiency Virus – the virus that can cause AIDS

immunity the body's ability to prevent infections by germs

infection when a germ grows inside the body and causes illness

placenta the barrier between the mother's and unborn baby's blood supply inside the mother's womb. It also supplies the baby with nutrients and oxygen from the mother

pneumonia an infection of the lungs

racism discrimination because of the color of someone's skin

STD Sexually Transmitted Disease

vaccine medical treatment given in a "jab" to boost immunity to other germs

vaginal intercourse sex in which a man's penis is put into a woman's vagina

virus a germ which can cause infection and which can multiply inside a living cell

INDEX

Photographic Credits

Cover and pages 13, 14, 15, 18, 25, 26, 28, 31, 44, 46, 47, 48, 54 and 59: Rex Features; page 4: Roger Vlitos; pages 6, 23, 39 and 49: Mike Goldwater/Network; pages 8, 36 and 58: Science Photo Library; pages 11 and 43: Geoff Franklin/Network; page 16: Hartman/Magnum Photos; page 30: Lighthouse Project; page 38: Manos/Magnum Photos; pages 41 and 56: Chris Steele-Perkins/ Magnum Photos; page 51: Lowe/Network.